FLIGHT PLAN

PEAK PERFORMANCE
in TURBULENT TIMES

DENNIS BAUER

For more information, for copies of this book, and to book Dennis Bauer for speaking engagements, visit www.DennisBauer.com or email Dennis@DennisBauer.com.

First Printing 2020
Printed in the United States of America
ISBN 978-0-578-72787-5

To Dad and to Mom who taught me the basics of getting from Point A to Point B whether mountain climbing, sailing, speaking, writing, starting and running a business, or flying airplanes. I will see you both again.

To my son DJ, who has proven himself in business and management excellence and is an excellent husband and dad. To my daughter Heather, with the grit to finish Ironman. Twice. And who does amazing things with hair. To my daughter Erin, creator of lovely things from used horseshoes. Entrepreneurship personified.

To everyone who faces The Unexpected.
Which is everyone.
This book is for you.

"There is bound to be turbulence in the clouds of confusion before one can view the friendly skies, and an illuminated landing strip."
—T. F. Hodge

CONTENTS

INTRODUCTION   1

CHAPTER 1 - PILOT IN COMMAND   7

CHAPTER 2 - PLANNING   19

CHAPTER 3 – WEIGHT & BALANCE   37

CHAPTER 4 – PREFLIGHT INSPECTION   51

CHAPTER 5 - TAKEOFF   59

CHAPTER 6 - CRUISE   67

CHAPTER 7 - NAVIGATION   79

CHAPTER 8 - COMMUNICATION   85

CHAPTER 9 – WHY WINGS BEND   97

CHAPTER 10 – BRING IT HOME   105

CHAPTER 11 - CONCLUSION   111

GO DEEPER, FARTHER, HIGHER...   115

IMAGINE THE NEXT STEP...   117

SPEAKING ENGAGEMENTS   119

ONLINE COURSES IN DEVELOPMENT...   121

WHAT NOW? FOLLOW ME AT...   123

Introduction

*A mile of road takes you a mile; a mile
of runway can take you anywhere!*

—anonymous

You can fly higher, go farther, and last longer than you think. Even in turbulent times, Peak Performance is your operational objective.

If that sounds like a positive affirmation to be posted on your bathroom mirror or refrigerator door, it is. And I affirm it for you, my friend!

Especially when you face turbulent times, having even one person cheering you on, telling you that you are amazing, and believing in you can make all the difference in accepting the challenges and handling them well.

You will read this book and get ideas that apply to your life, to your relationships, to your adventures, and to your business.

Whatever your endeavor—from building a relationship to building a business, from attempting to lose weight to busting your backside to build a $40 million business—you'll find a lot in Flight Plan that will help you toward Peak Performance.

About the Author

I love aviation. As a boy, you could give me no better birthday or Christmas gift than a model airplane. I slaved over trimming the plastic parts from the parts tree. I carefully applied the right amount of Tester's glue, patiently painted the cockpit and wings and fuselage, and lovingly applied the decals.

In the 6th grade, I found a book in the school library and read about learning to fly. There was a photo taken from inside the cabin of a small airplane flying over a city at night. And now, I have done that… and it truly is a great sight! I joined the United States Air Force Reserves and learned to fly while in tech school at Chanute Air Force Base in Rantoul, Illinois. Then came a Commercial Pilot certificate, an Instrument rating, and a Certified Flight Instructor certificate.

Later, when I started giving speeches, I discovered many analogies from the flying world that relate to life, to relationships, to business… to anything that involves getting from Point A to Point B.

To read about my unexpected experience of engine failure 5,000' off the ground of northern Colorado, and whether I survived or not, and the life and business lessons from that experience… get a copy *of Fumes and a Prayer: How to Live at the Edge and Still Be Home for Dinner* at DennisBauer.com/book. I'll even get you a signed copy!

I love airplanes, and I love flying them. I love stories, and I love lessons learned from them. And I love telling people about them and making a difference in the lives of people and their endeavors.

These lessons scale. The principles involved apply equally to small daily hopes and dreams, to the world of small business and giant corporations, to national and global events and even pandemics.

I hope this book makes a difference to you. If it does, I'd love to hear your story. Send me an email or come say hello at DennisBauer.com.

Full Power!

It takes full power to get an aircraft off the ground. Sometimes you have a long, wide runway in front of you with room for error. Other times, you're faced with a short, grassy runway with trees at the other end, and you'd better know what you're doing to ensure a safe takeoff.

If you want to get off the ground, you need motion. And you need to push the throttle full forward for maximum power.

Get Ready to Write It Down!

Read through this book in one sitting if you can, which at first reading should take you only about an hour.

Get yourself a journal dedicated to writing out your thoughts after reading each chapter. Then dig through the book slowly and thoughtfully, a chapter at a time. It will be gold! You are pursuing Peak Performance!

Enjoy these stories. Ponder the lessons. Implement your ideas. And then, on your way from Point A to Point B, go make a difference.

Are you ready for the journey?

"You are cleared for takeoff!"

Chapter 1

Pilot in Command

On a clear summer afternoon, my friend Sam and four other passengers climb into a high-wing, six-passenger, single-engine Cessna 206 at Gray Field. We want to see the ocean.

We are headed from Tacoma, Washington, to a small, paved airstrip at Ocean Shores on the Pacific Coast, a short, half-hour hop away.

I have the current weather briefing. I have a flight plan. I have figured the total weight and balance figures, and we are within published limits. I have topped off the fuel tanks. And I head along the taxiway for Runway 33 (pronounced "three-three").

"Gray Tower, Cessna 1065V, ready for takeoff, departing to the west." I coordinate my departure with the control tower. I'm the pilot, and I'm in command of my airplane, in command of every aspect of the flight—communication, navigation, safety of flight—everything!

"Cessna 1065V, Gray Tower, cleared for takeoff. Traffic is a helicopter one mile to the north."
"Gray Tower, Cessna 1065V, roger, cleared for takeoff, will watch for traffic."

I push the throttle full forward and accelerate along the dashed white runway centerline. I pull back on the controls, the nose obediently lifts off the runway, and we become airborne, climbing like an eagle lifting from its nest, eager to ascend higher and higher.

A half hour later, I turn south and begin our approach to Runway 24 at Ocean Shores.

There are two constant factors about landing at Ocean Shores. One is the industrial and retail buildings just before reaching the runway threshold.

The other is the wind. It's always windy at Ocean Shores, and the wind almost always crosses the runway at an angle so that I cannot just point the nose of the airplane straight down the runway as I approach for landing. Adding to the tension is the dynamic of the wind that swirls around and over those buildings. Handling the airplane on final approach can get tricky!

Still, I'm the pilot, and I have trained for this. I make constant adjustments to the flight controls so I can keep the wings level, my airspeed and my rate of descent accurate, and my flight path aligned with the runway.

As expected, I do get turbulence as I clear the buildings by a couple hundred feet, and it gets a bit squirrely.

I touch down a bit off the centerline and not exactly where I want to be... and a bit rough. I turn off the runway toward the parking ramp. I don't feel good about that landing.

"Sam," I say to my friend in the right seat, "that was *not* a pretty landing!"

"Hmph. *Any* landing you walk away from is a good landing." He quotes an aviation proverb, and I just shrug.

After some time on the beach, my passengers and I fly back to Gray Field, and this time I "grease" it on the runway. As I roll along the taxiway, I turn to Sam. "Now *that* was great landing!"

To which Sam pointedly replied, "Hmph! We haven't walked away yet."

But we did walk away. Later, I fill in my pilot's logbook, and in "Comments" I note the turbulence we encountered on the approach. In the column for airtime, I record 1 hour, 10 minutes as "Pilot in Command."

Pilot in Command. The captain of the ship. The "boss" (as a term of endearment used by Sir Ernest Shackleton's men on their polar expedition). The leader. The decision-maker, the responsibility-taker. The PIC. In aviation terms: Pilot in Command.

You are the PIC, the Pilot in Command of your venture. Whatever happens, you've got the controls in your hands, and you're ready for this.

So, let's talk about being "in command."

Leadership

This is a non-flying story, but it's a true story that involves a leadership role.

In my senior year in college, the president and the deans come up with a plan to divide the student body into four "houses" somewhat like the Greek system of fraternities and sororities. There aren't any orientation rituals and there aren't any frat houses. The goal is to promote spirit, esprit de corps, and unity.

Each house has a Greek name, though, and I am assigned to Phi Tau Kappa, "Lights of the World." Each house is to be involved in five aspects of student body life: Academics, Community Service, House Spirit, a Missions Project, and Intramural Sports.

Each house holds elections for officers, and on the day Phi Tau Kappa meets to elect officers, each candidate goes up in front of the large classroom and gives a short speech.

Those running for president go up last. There is only one candidate, reluctantly ambling to the front of the room.

He says something along the lines of, "I don't really care if I do this or not, but if you want me to, I guess I will. I guess we can do this, and, um, well, this could be fun, and, ah, maybe even helpful. So, let's all pull together and, um, see what happens."

For me, I've had leadership roles both before that time and since. But my style is not to jump at every chance I can to be the leader. If there's already a good leader, I'm happy to be a team player. Where there's an absence of leadership, especially in something I believe in, I step up.

And I see this as an absence of leadership. Plus, it is a system with a purpose I believe in.

A faculty member asks, "Are there any more candidates for president of Phi Tau Kappa?"

I raise my hand. I stride forward and deliver an impromptu speech about group esprit-de-corps, about a vision of team leaders for each of the five areas of endeavor, about developing as a college community, about helping our grade point averages as well as doing good things in our local community and even around the world.

I step up; I take the challenge. I get elected.

I am now the "pilot-in-command" of Phi Tau Kappa, and I prepare to do exactly what I'm about to teach you here in this book.

Our plan is formulated. I pull together a team of volunteers who will lead the five "departments" along with helpers for each team.

We meet regularly. First, we set objectives for our academics. The leader of that group suggests a visit to the Dean of Students to get statistics for where our house's current grade point average is, followed by visits to various faculty members for their input on how to raise our grades.

Leaders and helpers come forward for each of the other four areas, and the teams formulate their plans.

We are rolling down the runway, baby... throttles full forward!

I get approval from the administration to design and order five, huge, beautiful, trophy-case size trophies to be awarded at the end of the school year to the house that does the best job in each of the five areas. The winners will be determined by ballot from every student in the college, except for the academic award which, of course, is academic.

Phi Tau Kappa is an incredible group of men and women. They see the vision. They see the enthusiasm of their leaders. They may be inspired by a slight level of competitiveness, too!

As PIC, my job is to oversee everything... not necessarily to do everything. Along with my team, I too get involved in good study habits, in our community and mission projects, and in sports. On purpose, I give several inspirational, "We've got this!" speeches.

We regularly meet for updates, for systems checks, for data, and for recognition of progress in the right direction. We study hard, we play hard, we work hard.

At the end of the year, the student body meets in the school chapel. Up front are all five gleaming trophies waiting to be handed out.

The Dean of Students gives a nice speech about how well the year has gone, and he congratulates the student body for all its successes.

And then he hands out the trophies one by one.

"The winner of the Academic Trophy is... Phi Tau Kappa!"

Applause from the entire student body feels good as I walk forward like an Academy Award winner to claim the prize on behalf of my house.

Then…

"The winner of the Spirit Award is… Phi Tau Kappa!"

More applause and the warm and satisfying feeling of success. I claim that prize, too, for my house.

Then…

"The winner of the Community Project Award is… Phi Tau Kappa!"

Wow! This is really good because it represents the solid work, the planning, and the teamwork of my housemates.

Then…

"The winner of the Missions Project Award is… Phi Tau Kappa!"

I wonder what everyone is thinking. Is it like the Oscars when a blockbuster cleans up all the major awards? Truthfully, I start to feel a little uncomfortable, a bit embarrassed. But, yes, I still go up and claim our trophy.

And finally, the last award for Sports.

"The winner of the Intramural Sports Award goes to…

One of the other houses… finally! I am mostly relieved that someone else gets to go up front to get the last trophy.

Then, I graduate, but not before the president of the college walks with me down a dirt road near the campus and personally congratulates me on the success of Phi Tau Kappa.

In the several years that follow, the college merges with four other colleges in the Denver area and becomes a full-fledged university, so that I can now put on my resume that I'm a proud graduate of Colorado Christian University.

I tell you this story for two reasons.

One reason is to illustrate several points of leadership, of being the pilot-in-command of any venture.

The other reason is to illustrate that I'm not making stuff up. I practice what I preach, and while not every endeavor is successful, others are. So, I put this story out there for you as a personal example of how these lessons work for me in real life.

So, where are you the pilot in command? As a parent, or a PTA leader, or a church leader, or a sports team, or a business owner, or a mid-level manager?

Maybe it's something personal. You are PIC of your weight, your health, your spiritual life.

Leadership has many aspects, of course, and hundreds (thousands!) of books have been written on the subject. Here, I want to emphasize these six points:

1. As a leader – you bear the vision
2. As a leader – you establish the plan
3. As a leader – you take the responsibility
4. As a leader – you accept accountability
5. As a leader – you establish and rely on teamwork
6. As a leader – you offer encouragement and demonstrate spirit and attitude.

Now, open your journal.

Name some area where you are the PIC.

Next, list each of these six points of leadership and write out as much as you can under each of the six points.

1. My vision for this endeavor is:
2. My plan, as I see it now, is:
3. I am responsible for:

4. I am accountable to (maybe more than one person):
5. A) My team (or staff) is:

   B) Each team member is good at:
6. I will encourage and inspire by:

I congratulate you on taking the initiative to read Flight Plan. As you work through it, my goal is to offer you insights and ideas that will help you, the Pilot in Command, toward Peak Performance as you navigate through turbulent times, whether now or in the future.

Remember to send me your story!

Do this and…

Pursue Peak Performance!

Chapter 2
Planning

It was a dark and stormy night.

—Snoopy

Wait. No, it isn't stormy. But it is dark. Earlier in the day, I flew a four-seat Cessna 172 south to visit a friend in Oregon. Now I leave the Portland-Troutdale Airport, located on the banks of the Columbia River, and fly northbound toward Tacoma, Washington.

It is a nighttime flight in good weather, but nevertheless, quite dark.

My flight instructor, Jeff, told me something when we went up for my first night cross-country flight from Tacoma, northbound over Seattle (absolutely gorgeous at night with all the lights beneath you!) to Paine Field near Everett, Washington.

19

Jeff told me, "When flying at night, always have three 'extras':

1. Extra altitude
2. Extra fuel
3. Extra planning."

For my flight from Oregon to Washington, I follow his advice. First, instead of flying at the usual 4,500' above sea level that I would have flown on a clear day, I fly at 6,500'. I also have full fuel tanks.

And I have extra planning. Because this is before electronic navigation using iPads and iPhones and more, I use paper navigation charts called Sectionals, like road maps but for airplanes, and a Navigation Log with my planned altitude, airspeed, groundspeed, wind direction at my altitude, and the corresponding adjustment for the magnetic heading to fly, and checkpoints along the way.

I draw a line on the nav chart for my direct route to the north.

FAA Aviation Sectional Chart

Sample Navigation Log Form

The magnetic heading on my plan is 327°, roughly north-northwest. I fly that heading as planned.

Flying can get boring, actually, especially when you reach your altitude and everything in the cockpit is set for straight-and-level flight. So, there is a rather long and monotonous segment after I leave the Portland area and climb to altitude. Everything is set.

The challenge is darkness, and I can no longer see the horizon. The blackness of the rural countryside below me and of the moonless night sky above blends into something like a dark room in the middle of the night when the lights are off and there's no nightlight.

Flying in the darkness certainly leaves me feeling disorientated. I mainly use my instruments for this dark part of the flight. And I use my compass to make sure I head toward my destination.

I know that at some point the lights of Olympia will begin to glow in the distant sky up ahead. But...

Ahead, and to my left, is the glow of the city.

"Wait a minute," I think. "That should be straight ahead of me, not over there."

And just like that, I become navigationally disoriented. Confused!

I look at my compass. It indicates that I am pointed in the right direction. It says I am on course per my plan.

I am sure something has gone wrong. Everything in me wants to turn the airplane left—to turn toward that distant glow which is my destination.

My instincts say, "Bauer, turn this airplane left. Right now!"

My head says, "Bauer, follow your plan!"

An internal, confusing conversation takes place about my destination, now obviously to my left.

Or… is it?

I pull out my chart and the planning form. Yes, I am supposed to fly a magnetic course of 327°, and yes, that's exactly what my instruments show that I am doing.

But then… when I look at the nav chart again, more closely, under the red cabin overhead light, I see to the left of my course, about 16 miles away, the town of… Kelso.

So *that's* where the glow on the horizon is coming from. Kelso. Not Olympia. Olympia *is* still straight ahead.

I stick to the plan. And eventually the glow of the night lights of Olympia appear on the horizon directly ahead of me.

In my logbook that night, I simply record a night flight in the Cessna 172 from Troutdale to Tacoma. There are no other remarks

I had a plan from the beginning of my journey, and I stuck to the plan. Then, when it looked like I was off course, I referred back to the plan and I verified that I was still headed to where I wanted to be, even though for a few minutes it did not at all feel like it.

I have never planned a flight that went exactly as planned from takeoff to landing.

The Principles

Making and following a plan scales from everyday to-do lists (plant a vegetable garden) to business endeavors involving millions of dollars (build a hangar for the new company airplane) to international crises (send aid to earthquake victims). The principles are the same:

1. Make a plan
2. Write it down
3. Implement it.

It takes all three to achieve Peak Performance. This is true for every endeavor, although the complexity of the plan will scale to the complexity of the endeavor.

You've heard some people say they operate this way :

1. Ready
2. Fire
3. Aim

rather than the traditional:

1. Ready
2. Aim
3. Fire.

And yet, notice that in whichever order you like to do things, whether you like to Fire and Aim, or Aim and Fire, both ways start with "Ready."

That's what this chapter is about. Be *ready* with your plan.

Let's begin with naming your endeavor. Write it down, maybe in a journal or in a notebook or even just a notepad if the project is a small one.

There are six parts to a plan:

1. Where you want to go. Point B.
2. Where you are right now. Point A.
3. How you will get from Point A to Point B.
4. What you will need to get there (assets, resources, abilities, talents, gifts, experiences).
5. What obstacles or challenges might stand in your way?
6. What is your timeline from Point A to Point B (and all points between)?

Do this as an exercise. You will get an enormous amount of benefit from writing it out. Don't skim the surface. The deeper you go, and the more detail you write, the more effective this will be and the more successful you will be in handling anything unexpected.

Your aim, after all, is Peak Performance.

Here are some ideas and examples:

1.   Where I want to go (Point B):

Write this out in present tense, as if you're already there. Take whatever time you need.

Business example:
At this time next year,
1. I am bringing in 20% more gross month-by-month.
2. I have an additional salesperson to handle fieldwork.
3. My expenses are reduced by 5%.
4. I am working five days a week instead of the current six days.
5. Because I've made more money, I have saved enough to take my dream vacation, and the business will run just fine while I'm gone.

Personal example:
In five months, I weigh 10 pounds less than I do today, and I can run a 5K marathon.

2. Where I am right now (Point A):

Business example:
I'm running a business that is stagnant. It's OK, and I'm making ends meet, but I know I could do better. I am at a place where I want more clients so I can improve my cash flow.

Personal example:
I weigh ___ pounds right now, I eat what I want, and I get no exercise. That's a lot of calorie intake, and I burn only whatever it takes to sit in a chair for several hours, eat meals, and sleep. Oh… and watch TV.

3. How I will get there:

Business example:
1. I will clarify and write out who my ideal client is.
2. I will research potential market areas so I can expand my sphere of influence.
3. I will research and hire a virtual assistant to maintain the website and the CRM software.
4. I will calendarize the steps of the marketing and sales processes.

5. I will spend two hours each workday making personal sales calls to new prospects.
6. I will begin to print out and study my monthly cash flow and P&L statements.
7. I will develop a simple way to keep track of receipts
8. I will upgrade the tools I need for the jobs I do.
9. I will ask for testimonials from happy customers, and I will use them online and in marketing pieces.

Personal example:
1. I will start today by keeping a log of how many calories I consume each day, meal-by-meal and snack-by-snack.
2. I will start today by walking 30-60 minutes five days each week.
3. In four weeks, I will start jogging, and I will increase the distance a few blocks every week until I can jog a 5K non-stop.

4.   What I will need to get there:

Business example:

1. Cash to pay for a part-time virtual assistant.
2. An updated website.
3. A series of pitches and sales letters written out. I will read a book (like Pitch Anything by Oren Klaff).

Personal example:
1. A journal to record my daily calorie intake and my daily walks/jogs.
2. A new pair of walking/jogging shoes.
3. A comfortable outfit, including rain gear for drizzly days.
4. Limit TV time to an hour each day.

5. What obstacles and/or challenges might stand in my way:

Business example:

1. I might need to work a few extra hours each week to make personal calls and send emails to new prospects because I don't have the cash to pay a virtual assistant at the moment.
2. Others on my team may not have the experience or training they need to make this happen.

Personal example:

1. I might have down days when I don't feel like exercising.
2. I might get sick sometime in this process.
3. I might get a sweet tooth sometimes and "cheat". A little bit. Maybe.

6.   What is my timeline from Point A to Point B (and all points between)?

Business example:

1. I will clarify and write out who my ideal client is.
   - Start Monday, finish same day
2. I will research potential market areas so I can expand my sphere of influence.
   - Start Tuesday, spend 3 days on this, finish Thursday
3. I will research and hire a virtual assistant to maintain the website and the CRM software.
   - Do research on Friday, hire on Monday
4. I will calendarize the steps of the marketing and sales processes.
   - Spend full day on Tuesday
5. I will spend two hours each workday making personal sales calls to new prospects.
   - Start Wednesday, continue M-F thereafter
6. I will begin to print out and study my monthly cash flow and P&L statements.
   - Calendarize a day each month to do previous month
7. I will develop a simple way to keep track of receipts.

- Next Monday morning
8. I will upgrade the tools I need for the jobs I do.
   - Start a list Next Tuesday, add to list as needed, finish list next Friday. Following Monday, start acquisitions
9. I will ask for testimonials from happy customers, and I will use them online and in marketing pieces.
   - In two weeks, compile list over two-day period. On 3rd day, compose emails. On 4th day, send emails.

Personal example:

1. I will start today by keeping a log of how many calories I consume each day, meal-by-meal and snack-by-snack.
   - Make a log in my journal this afternoon. Start tracking tomorrow morning for the next 28 days.
2. I will start today by walking 30-60 minutes five days each week.
   - This afternoon, I will walk. I will record it in my journal.

3. In four weeks, I will start jogging, and I will increase the distance a few blocks every week until I can jog a 5K non-stop.

    -   After 28 days of walking, I will start jogging. I will record it in my journal. Tomorrow I will research and find a 5K in my area that will occur in 6 months. That is my target date.

Sounds good! Now what?

Now, write it out for yourself.

Seriously (I can't emphasize this enough!), write it all out. Doing this clearly and completely will give you your best shot at handling the inevitable turbulence you will encounter on your journey.

1. Where I want to go.
2. Where I am right now.
3. How I plan to get there.
4. What I will need to get there.
5. What obstacles or challenges might stand in my way?
6. What is my timeline from Point A to Point B?

It's too hard to keep very much of a plan in your head. For me, if I'm sent to the grocery store for more than three things, I need to write it down.

On a little more complex level than the grocery list, I have a goal of building my own airplane. This is going to take two or three years if all goes according to plan. I started my planning with research to know which one I want to build and to see if it was feasible.

Then I looked at where I'm at right now: I need some space about the size of a garage, I need a lot of tools I don't currently own, and I need enough cash to start the first kit (the tail section).

I have mapped out on paper the progression of steps to take, and I've set deadlines to finish each section. Obstacles standing in my way might be: cash flow, building time into my daily and weekly schedule, and finding the space to work on it.

You might have a business or a project worth hundreds of thousands of dollars or more, and your planning will take a lot of pages, maybe even notebooks and file cabinets. The principles are still the same.

I personally use two Rocketbooks and a journal I designed called *LOGBOOK: A Personal Journey* for brainstorming and handwriting plans. It's a journal, plus sections for working out projects, problems, schedules, and more, and a very handy and helpful index system.

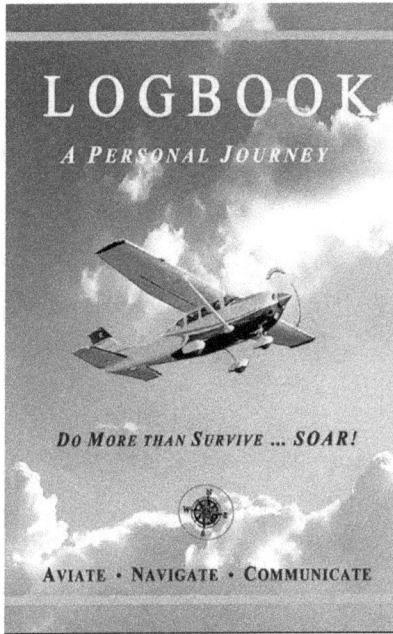

LOGBOOK

A Personal Journey

Do More than Survive ... SOAR!

Aviate · Navigate · Communicate

The LOGBOOK is available at DennisBauer.com/logbook.

Use whatever works for your planning, whether personal or business. The rewards of doing this monumentally outweigh just flying by the seat of your pants.

Do this, and…

Pursue Peak Performance!

Chapter 3
Weight and Balance

A pilot who flew the jungles of Papua New Guinea for a missionary organization was asked to deliver an anvil to a remote location.

Now, there is a forward and aft limit for each airplane that sets the limit for where the weight may safely be distributed. If too much weight is forward of this safe area, then the airplane will be nose heavy and either unable to get off the ground or unable to maintain anything other than a descent.

On the other hand, if too much weight is behind that area, the airplane will be tail heavy and will be unable to fly very well, if at all.

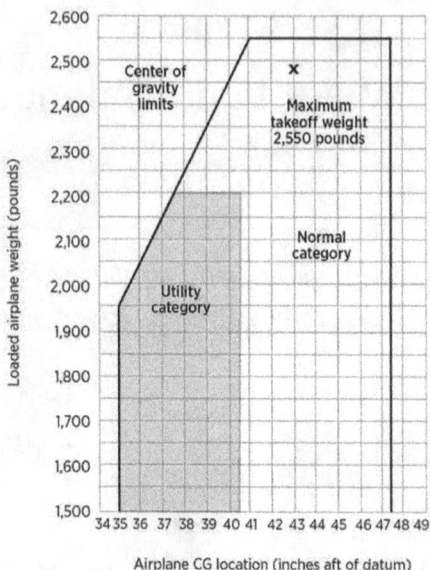

Sample Weight & Balance Graph

The missionary pilot loaded the anvil into the airplane within the weight-and-balance limits and took off to deliver the anvil.

Having decided that the anvil was so heavy it could not possibly slide on the floor of the cabin, he did not tie it down. When he took off from the runway, he pulled back on the control wheel, and the nose came up as it should. But then…

As he climbed into the air with the nose skyward, the unsecured anvil *did* slide backward, past the aft limit for weight and balance, putting far too much weight in the tail section—so much so that the airplane could no longer fly, and it fell backwards to earth, wrecking the plane and killing the pilot.

Every pilot is trained to check the weight and balance of the aircraft before leaving the parking ramp. If you load too much weight, you won't get off the ground, or, at best, you might have enough lift to get the wheels off the runway but not enough to climb. That can be disastrous.

I've heard of corporate pilots telling business executives that they can't take everything they brought for the trip…leave it behind or else wait for the fuel truck to arrive to suck out some of the fuel right there on the parking ramp in order to reduce the weight the airplane has to carry.

Here are the lessons from the story.

First, there is a limit as to how much you can carry. There are only so many hours in a day, only so many days in a week, and so on. And some of those hours you need for sleep so your brain can keep working like it's supposed to and so your body doesn't get sick. You must set your boundaries… and be realistic about it.

Think this through, make some decisions about your limits and boundaries, and, again, write them down.

Another area involves cash flow. I teach that there are two basics to business. There is more to business than these two basics, like there's more to golf than "just hit the ball," as my friend used to tell me. But if you don't hit the ball, you have no game.

And if you don't have these two basics, you have no business... not for long, anyway.

These are the two basics of business:

1. Quality of product or service
2. Cash flow.

I'll make just one point on this. Cash flow is to your business what blood is to your body. When it stops flowing, you die. Quickly.

By cash flow, I do not mean how much cash you have on hand. You can get investors or get loans to put money in the bank. That's not cash flow, that's just a cash asset, like a man-made pond that was filled once but that has neither a natural source nor outlet.

That is cash on hand. But it is not cash *flow*.

Here's the rule of healthy, positive cash flow:

Do not spend more than you make.

Know the difference between cash-on-hand and cash flow. The basic rule of cash flow is:
Do not spend more than you make!

If you are currently out of balance on cash flow, you need to do a weight-and-balance check. Do you need more income to balance the expenses? Or do you need to reduce expenses to match the income?

Either way, you must be fiercely adamant about this. Set your limits and stick to them. Reach for Peak Performance in your finances. Keep records and record and review them regularly, then make any adjustments necessary to maintain positive cash flow.

There's another lesson from the story. Some things are less stable than you think they are, and it is easy to get blindsided by something unexpected. The pilot assumed the anvil was stable, that it would not move. But when the physical situation changed, and the airplane started to climb, things changed suddenly and dramatically.

A good friend of mine had his business for over thirty years. He was successful... not getting wealthy, but able to support his family, buy a home, and live comfortably. He was well-liked by his employees, and he had positive testimonials from happy clients.

His office ran smoothly and, because he enjoyed the hands-on part of his business, he was frequently away from the office. His office work was handled by a secretary plus a trusted relative who did the bookkeeping and kept track of taxes and insurance.

While not idyllic, life was good for my friend. But then...

The unexpected hit him hard—like turbulent winds swirling and surrounding his business—when it was discovered that the bookkeeper had embezzled around $100,000 from the company, had kept for himself funds that were meant to cover insurance and taxes, and spent most of that money on personal items. Turbulent, indeed!

First, my friend was out of cash. Then the insurance company came after him for an auto accident involving a company van and which was completely the other driver's fault. He had trusted his bookkeeper to pay the bills, but since the insurance hadn't been paid for some time, he was no longer covered.

Then the IRS came after him because his employee taxes had not been paid. For three years! The IRS put a lien on his home.

While I'm happy for my friend that arrangements were finally made with the IRS to pay the back taxes, I'm sad that he had to sell his business.

In my mind, he made one major mistake. He did not check the essentials of his business, which became evident when it was too late, and he lost it all. His business was out of balance and he didn't know it. And his business crashed.

Every Pilot in Command of an aircraft is ultimately responsible for everything about the flight—the planning, the weather, weight-and-balance, the route, the condition of passengers, the fuel load— everything!

Make sure you check. Tie down the "anvils"— those things that are essential both to keep your business running and to fulfill your mission— and make secure whatever you need to.

There's this from a proverb in ancient Scripture: "Be sure you know the condition of your flocks, give careful attention to your herds." NIV

Here's how I learned this the hard way:

I owned a small video production company for ten years—back in the videotape days. A couple of years into the business, I somewhat accidentally got into videotaping figure skating competitions.

I did a couple of local competitions for a friend, but he did not want to expand outside his local area.

So, when competition directors saw that people liked the way our videos turned out, I picked up more and more local competitions throughout the Northwest until I had about 95% of the market share in Washington, Oregon, Idaho, and Alaska.

This was a family-run, mom-and-pop-and-kids business, and often all five of us drove to wherever the competition was.

As our reputation spread and my marketing increased, competitions were picked up around the country. We drove from the Pacific Northwest as far away as Colorado Springs, Boston, and Tampa Bay.

I was getting sectional, regional, and national-level competitions. These involved a lot of planning: Estimating how many tapes we would need and ordering them, arranging for additional camera crew if needed and renting extra equipment for the larger events, planning travel and budgets, printing order forms, and making calls back and forth with the competition directors.

Because I was contracted by the event committees as a vendor, there was always a risk. My on-site sales alone determined how much money we made. But I always made at least a little bit, and sometimes a lot, so the risk was mitigated by my experiences of success at every competition.

About three years into doing these jobs, I applied for and won the exclusive rights to be the official videographer for the USFSA World Championships in Boston, Massachusetts.

A full month of preparation led to all five of us driving across Interstate 90 to Boston where I had a total crew of five videographers and nine order table salespeople. DJ and Heather, my son and oldest daughter, ran video cameras stationed rink-side and recorded every skater, all day long, for five days straight, covering two of the four sheets of ice that had simultaneous events. My younger daughter, Erin, oversaw the order tables, video printers, and the sales team.

We were busy! And it wasn't easy.

Mid-week, the facility ran out of food at the concession stand where we, along with all the skaters and parents, bought our meals. We got hungry! The facility ordered a lot of pizza which was delivered that afternoon. But then

The next morning, many skaters were sick, and Heather and a couple of my crew got food poisoning. Still, they worked through the upset stomachs and did their jobs and did them well. I was impressed!

At the end of the week, we counted about 1,000 orders with a total of over 3,000 individual and group events to be copied one-by-one onto customer tapes. We celebrated!

In appreciation, I bought nice varsity-style leather jackets for every team member and took all fourteen of them out for a genuine East Coast lobster dinner at Kennedy's Pub in Marlboro, Massachusetts.

In one week, my little video production company grossed $44,000! Amazing!

The fulfillment process took three full months and involved an editing crew of three people.

The following year, I got the contract again for the USFSA World Championships, this time in St. Louis, and this one covered five sheets of ice at three locations around the city. Again, five straight days with a camera crew, order table crew, extra equipment rented, and so on.

And in St. Louis, I made $40,000 in one week. Phenomenal! But then...

After St. Louis and the several months of order fulfillment, I noticed my business bank account no longer reflected the financial success of that week in St. Louis. I'd noticed the same thing after Boston the previous year, but I wasn't broke, so I paid no attention. (You see where this is going, yes?)

Confused about where all that money went, I sat down and did what I should have done immediately after Boston. If I had, I would not have gone to St. Louis.

I put all the numbers from the event into a P&L spreadsheet and included every expense—even the cost of my time for the month of preparation, the two weeks for the event including travel, and the three months of order fulfillment.

Sure enough, on the Income side, things had been very bright. So bright, in fact, that I didn't notice the expenses.

But I should have looked! Because when all was said and done, and after I took a good look at the numbers, my grand total net from St. Louis was a meager $1,500.

So, I ran the numbers from Boston. Amazing! Same outcome.

And that's how I learned the importance of keeping track of my financial reports to verify the health of my business. I was winging it, and that wasn't enough.

Lesson learned! Not as life-threatening as forgetting to tie down an anvil in a small airplane, but just as unwise.

You are the Pilot in Command of your business or endeavor. Just like a pilot who checks the weight and balance charts before a flight, you must make the decision right now that you will keep track of your reports:

1. If you haven't set up your financial record-keeping system yet, decide on a time when you will do it, or when you will hire someone to do it for you.
2. Write on your calendar at least one day each month when you will check your numbers.
3. Decide on a place where you keep your receipts and invoices as well as any other records you need to track.

Keep your endeavor alive. Know your numbers.

Do this, and…

Pursue Peak Performance!

Chapter 4

Preflight Inspection

By failing to prepare, you are preparing to fail.

—Benjamin Franklin

Every single flight I've made since my very first flight lesson has started exactly the same way.

It was Day One, a balmy September day in LaGrande, Oregon, and I walked out with Jeff, my flight instructor, to a machine that sat on three wheels and under a pair of wings, and which would, in a few minutes, carry us skyward.

The two-seat, white airplane with a yellow and a brown stripe along the side, sat soaking in the sunshine waiting for us to take the controls and make wonderful things happen. Like, overcome gravity.

My first flight lesson started with a half-hour of instruction on the ground as Jeff showed me how to do a preflight inspection of the airplane.

(You can read about that flight, and others, in my book, Fumes and a Prayer: How to Live at the Edge and Still Be Home for Dinner, which you can get at www.DennisBauer.com/book. Or look on Amazon if you'd like to download a Kindle edition.)

Teaching the parts of an airplane and how to preflight it is the first lesson I've given to every student I've had.

In my 20s, my goal was to fly overseas as a jungle pilot for a missionary organization. That job required not only advanced pilot certificates but also airplane mechanic licenses. I went to nearly two years of school for my Airframe and Powerplant Mechanic tickets.

In airplane mechanic school, one of the instructors told us this true story:

There was a pilot who owned his own airplane. The rudder of his plane needed a repair, so the pilot left his plane at a shop where an experienced aircraft mechanic took the rudder off the airplane to make the repairs.

A few days later the pilot returned to the shop. The mechanic wasn't there, and the pilot wanted to take his airplane out and go flying. He pulled the airplane out of the hangar with a manual tow bar.

Then he climbed into the pilot's seat, taxied away from the hangars, lined up his aircraft with the nose pointed straight down the runway, released the brakes, pushed the throttle full forward for maximum power, and pulled back on the control wheel to point the nose of the airplane up over the horizon.

This would be a nice day for a flight.

But it wasn't.

No sooner had he left the ground than he lost control of the airplane and crash-landed.

And here's why.

The rudder had not been installed back onto the airplane. It was still back on the mechanic's workbench.

I have yet to meet a pilot who hears the story and isn't amazed at the apparent negligence (stupidity!) of the pilot that day. How can you miss the fact that your rudder is missing!?

That fact would have been more than obvious to him if only he had completed a preflight inspection or even just walked around his airplane with his eyes open. You just could not miss it!

But he didn't do it, and he crashed. Fortunately for him, he survived. And he sued the mechanic. And he won. (I know! What?) A jury decided that the mechanic should have put a note in the cockpit of the airplane so the pilot would be notified of the missing rudder. But again, every pilot I know who hears the story just shakes their head.

The purpose of a preflight inspection is to make sure the airplane is "airworthy", that it is legal and capable of flight… *before* you try to take this machine off the ground.

In the flying world, this means that before every flight, you as the pilot do the following:

1. Check the paperwork that authorizes the plane to fly. Check the engine and airframe logbooks for maintenance updates, and to see that the appropriate inspections are up to date for the aircraft and its avionics. There are seven documents involved in this plus several inspection records.

2. Evaluate the aircraft's condition. This a walk-around, physical inspection of the condition of the aircraft including (but not limited to) all surfaces, moving parts, hinges and connection points, visual check of the fuel level, tires and brakes, antennae, and more.

3. Evaluate himself. Is he or she safe mentally, emotionally, and physically to fly at that moment?

Pilots have an acronym for this:

IM SAFE

I – Illness – am I sick?
M – Medication – am I taking medications?
S – Stress – am I under undue stress?
A – Alcohol – has it been at least eight hours?
F – Food – have I eaten?
E – Emotions – am I upset? Angry? Irritated?

I want a positive answer to each of those in order to pass a preflight inspection of myself as the pilot.

The FAA says that "The owner/operator is primarily responsible for maintenance, but the pilot is (solely) responsible for determining the airworthiness (and/or safety) of the airplane for flight." (Airplane Flying Handbook, chapter 2).

Now, how did you preflight your year? How did you preflight your day?

When you began your endeavor this morning, what was the first thing you did?

Personally, I start most mornings with about an hour of reading the Bible, meditating on what I've read, praying, and journaling. For me, that sets the tone for the day and helps put my personal and business plans into a bigger perspective. Not a bad place to start. If you're not doing that, give it a try.

Ed Rush is a mentor to me, and he begins his workday by first looking at his bank accounts. That's a good place to start if you want to see that income is there and that a "damaged rudder" is not missing somewhere that will cause you trouble if not fixed.

The lesson here is that, like a pilot, you check everything about your endeavor—that it is prepared and safe, that you can expect Peak Performance because you know that everything about your endeavor is operational and working as it should.

In *LOGBOOK: A Personal Journey*, you'll find several unique features. There is a section for recording your plans, goals, and thoughts for the next twelve months—what you want your endeavor to look like twelve months from now. Then there is a section to do the same for each quarter of the next year, and for each month of the year. It's spiral bound so it lays flat for conveniently writing in it.

The critical key, as always, is to *write it down*. You get clarity, direction, and hope when you write these things down.

Treat this like a preflight inspection. You *must* do this before you take off—before you start the next twelve month's journey, and the next quarter, the next month, the next week, and even the next day.

1. Get the LOGBOOK or similar planner or journal.
2. List each aspect and system of your endeavor. (marketing, sales, accounting, operations, fitness schedule, etc.)
3. Regularly do a "preflight". Review each aspect and system of your endeavor. What's the status of your records? What's the status of your communications? What's the status of your moving parts (marketing letters, sales, phone or email contacts…)?
4. Put that on your calendar!

Go to the bookstore or look online for a tool you like and that you will use.

You can get *LOGBOOK: A Personal Journey* by visiting me at DennisBauer.com/logbook.

Do this, and…

Pursue Peak Performance!

Chapter 5

Takeoff

The universe is full of noise. True wisdom is in knowing what to pay attention to.

—Debasish Mridha

"**D**ecatur Tower, Cessna 12345, ready to taxi to the active for takeoff northeast bound."

"Cessna 12345, Decatur Tower, taxi to Runway Six via Taxiway Alpha."

I'm the pilot in a two-seat, Cessna trainer airplane. I have a newly issued Private Pilot certificate burning a hole in my wallet, and I have made my first flight with a passenger—a very big day for a pilot!—from Chanute Air Force Base near Rantoul, Illinois, where I am in tech school. They have a flying club there, and that's where I trained to become a pilot.

My passenger is, in fact, a cute young instructor at the tech school, and all the guys want to get a date with her. She turns them all down. But when I invite her to go flying with me, she accepts! I'm not sure what, exactly, to make of that, but I feel pretty good about it when the other guys find out.

So far, the flight has been uneventful despite my first-time-with-a-passenger jitters, and my passenger seems duly impressed with my aviation prowess. I have no intention of being a show-off in an airplane—I just want everything to go right so that I can impress her with the fact that I can make everything go right!

After a brief stop at the airport pilots' lounge and then doing another preflight check, we are back in the little airplane. I fire up the engine and receive the tower's instructions to taxi to Runway 6. What a nice day I'm having!

Near the intersection of Runway 6 and Runway 36, I perform my pre-takeoff check. Everything is perfect, so I call the tower.

"Decatur Tower, Cessna 12345, ready for takeoff."

"Cessna 12345, Decatur Tower, you are cleared for takeoff, Runway 6."

A quick glance at the cute young passenger, a confident smile and thumbs up as if I was an old-time pilot with leather helmet and goggles and a scarf around my neck, and I power up to turn on to the "active" runway. The takeoff is so smooth!

Then, unexpectedly...
"Cessna 12345, Decatur Tower, where the **** are you headed?!!!"

Ummmm...

"Cessna 12345, you were cleared for Runway 6. You took off on Runway 36!"

All this comes over the cabin speaker, and there is no hiding the authoritative, irritated, and condescending tone in the controller's voice. I have no words. My cockiness evaporates. I am deflated. In the presence of the cute young tech school instructor.
Then I realize my error.

The beginning of Runways 6 and 36 converge—each runway begins at practically the same point on the airport. Plus, the numbers 6 and 36 are easy to confuse, especially if I was not focused on the numbers painted on the runway, which, apparently, I was not.

Decatur Airport Diagram.
Note Runways 3 and 36 in the lower right corner.

Perhaps I was distracted.

Anyway, the cute young instructor did not go flying with me again.

Pilot workload is great during takeoff. When the brakes are released and the throttle is pushed full forward, the pilot becomes both highly alert and active.

There is radio contact with the tower, a check of the compass, maintaining directional control using the rudder pedals, awareness of the direction and strength of any wind across the runway and making appropriate adjustments with the ailerons so a wing doesn't lift up on one side, keeping constant attention on the airspeed indicator as the airspeed increases to takeoff-decision speeds, checking for other aircraft who might be mistakenly on, or about to be on, or are crossing the active runway...

And that's *before* the airplane lifts off the ground! It all continues as the aircraft climbs out and away from the airport.

The FAA reports that one out of five aircraft accidents occur in the takeoff and climb portion of the flight, and more than half of those are because of pilot error and loss of control.

How important it is, then, to be very alert when *you* apply full power to *your* endeavor. You've prepared your plan, you've made sure you know your limits and are operating within them, you've checked all the parts of your endeavor, and they're in working order... and now you push the throttle full forward.

Ready for takeoff!

Right there in that space lies the potential for disaster. Distractions can take you down. In my experience, in any endeavor from taking off on a new fitness program to tackling a new class or course to taking a vacation, to climbing a mountain... Enemy #1 is Distraction.

In flying, when we need to focus, we use a term for the takeoff and landing phases of flight: Sterile cockpit. That means no one talks unless necessary for the performance and safety of the procedure. No conversations. No personal remarks. No distractions!

Distractions can take you down. Enemy #1 is Distraction. Especially at the start of your endeavor, distraction can take you off course—or worse.

Whether you are a parent or a student, or a small business owner (or *any* size business owner), or the CEO of a major international corporation—distraction, especially at the start of your endeavor, can cause you to go off course—or worse.

Here's a very important exercise for you.

Write this out:

1. Name your endeavor, your project, or your startup.

2. List the things that have distracted you in the recent past. Google searches? TV? Email? Social media? You name it. List as many as you can think of and try to be honest and transparent about this.

3. Then list the things that come to mind that might distract you as you begin your new project. Take several minutes at least to write these out.

4. At the bottom of the page, write this:

"These distractions are my enemies! I will fight them off like a warrior! And I will win! I am the Pilot in Command here. I am focused like a laser. I do not allow these things I've listed to distract me from my endeavor nor to detract from the efforts I'm about to make."

Then... do it!

Do this, and…

Pursue Peak Performance!

Chapter 6

Cruise

Life does not get better by chance, it gets better by change.

—Jim Rohn

On a sunny, June afternoon my girlfriend and I plan a flight from the Aurora State Airport in western Oregon to the Ken Jernstedt Airfield near Hood River Oregon. We want a scenic flight along the Columbia River Gorge and a quiet lunch when we arrive.

The takeoff goes as planned, as does the climb to our cruise altitude about 1,500' above the sparkling Columbia River. The flight includes views of Multnomah Falls, and 75 other waterfalls, plus Crown Point, Vista House, the Bonneville Dam... oh my! It will be a beautiful flight, for sure! But...

There is wind, and a lot of it, coming through the Gorge— magnified by the narrowing of the surrounding Cascade Mountains on either side of the Gorge. Wind by itself isn't so bad in flight, but here, the wind swirls and ebbs and flows like water does in rapids and narrow river passages. And we bounce around. A lot!

I am calm. Experience helps with that. My passenger, not very experienced in small aircraft like the four-seat Piper Warrior we are in, grabs my arm—with an accompanying yelp—at every bump and bounce of the airplane. We are buffeted by the winds for a long thirty minutes, thankful at least for tightly secured seat belts and shoulder harnesses.

I try to take a video of the beauty and majesty of the Gorge, but the result looks as if I am riding a bucking bronco!

So much for a happy passenger. So much for an enjoyable, scenic flight.

I wonder what the landing will be like.

"Flying is 99% pure boredom.
The other 1% is sheer terror!"
—old pilots' saying

This chapter is about being ready to handle the part of your journey when you are in cruise mode and unexpected things make it desirable, or even imperative, to make changes to your plan.

The Boring 99% Part

Most endeavors are going to involve times of tedium. That's a dangerous time because it can lull you into complacency. And drowsiness.

In November 2018, an Australian pilot flew a twin-engine airplane from Devenport, Tasmania, to King Island in Bass Strait, a flight of about an hour and twenty minutes. He fell asleep with the autopilot engaged, and he overflew the King Island airport by about 29 miles before waking up, turning the airplane around, and flying back to King Island Airport.

When things get humdrum, or you get fatigued, this is the danger you must avoid. Danger becomes imminent. Vigilance becomes imperative. The longer the road you've been on, the easier it is to become complacent or even to fall asleep at the wheel.

As the miles or hours or days seem to drag on, it becomes vital for you to be rested and alert and to maintain a vigilant watch on your instruments and your flight plan, cross-checking your data, looking ahead for a clear path toward Point B.

You see the metaphor there.

On a personal level, let's say you want to lose weight. Point B is a future number you want to see when you step on the scale. The distance between Point A, your current weight, and Point B, your target weight, usually takes time and patience. On the journey, the endeavor can get tedious, boring, and even discouraging, as those who've done it can attest to.

Any endeavor that requires grit will be like that, and you just don't quit. There are no magic pills. Endurance and resilience are simply two qualities that you develop over time and which you will need for that 99%.

If it gets really boring at work, take a class or read a good business book, get a friend involved, put positive affirmations on your bathroom mirror and on your refrigerator.

Do not fall asleep at the wheel. That is the only reason the fabled hare lost to the incredibly slow (and probably boring) tortoise. Stay awake, even if it's just you, all alone, plodding along the beaten path.

How serious are you about getting to Point B? Keep your goal in mind always. Remember why you're on this road anyway! Imagine yourself crossing the finish line. Picture that Point B as you recorded it in Chapter Two, Planning.

Stay alert! You've got this. Keep going. You'll get there! You are AMAZING!

The 1% Terror Part

Hopefully "terror" overstates your response to any challenge, change, or circumstance you may face, but you get the point. You get hit hard, head-on, by The Unexpected.

For example:

In business:
- Discovery of embezzlement
- Parts not delivered on time
- Wrong parts delivered
- Vendor/sub-contractor delayed
- Accident
- Changes in government policy or restriction
- Failure to receive payment
- Losing clients to another company

In personal life:
- Illness
- Unexpected visit from relatives
- Accident
- Losing a job
- Needs of family members
- Unexpected visit from the IRS
- Surprise bills

- Death of a dear pet
- Breakup of a relationship

What you really need is to stay calm. Your team needs you to stay calm. The success of your endeavor depends on you staying calm.

Two things help you stay calm:

1. **Hope** – your vision of a likely and positive outcome.
2. **Experience** – your vision of past successes and lessons learned that apply to your current circumstance.

That "1% terror" part for a pilot simply means that things have gotten a little out of hand. The engine quits. The weather turns ugly. An instrument fails.

Though not complacent, you stay calm. You have experienced this before, in practice flights at least. And you have hope because you see how you fix the problem, restart the engine, rely on other instruments, or make a safe emergency landing.

The weather gets bumpy and you wish for smoother air, but you've been through this before and nothing bad happened. And you know there is smoother air ahead. Or up higher. Or down lower.

You prevent panic first by gaining, and then remembering, your experiences, and then by looking ahead at an outcome that you can expect—as long as you keep moving toward it.

It's easy to tell someone to stay calm, isn't it? But when it's you, remember your training and experiences and apply that to your present circumstance. Then, if you can, write out the outcome you want to see down the road.

Make any appropriate changes in light of your experiences and your desired outcome.

Sometimes, just changing altitude will give a pilot (and passengers) a smoother ride.

We continue the bouncy ride toward Hood River. The airport itself is nestled between hills and, like the gorge, on a windy day, those hills create wind patterns that are unpredictable.

Approaching the airport traffic pattern at 1,000' above the ground, I go through the checklist for approach and landing and then fly the downwind leg, about a half-mile away from and parallel to the runway, and we do bounce around quite a bit.

Toward the end of that leg, I reduce power a bit in order to begin the descent. After a turn to the left for the base leg perpendicular to the runway, I turn again to the left and line up with Runway 25 for the final approach… and continue the bouncy descent.

I can do this. I've done it many times before. But then…

These last moments on short final become very interesting indeed. And turbulent.

With only seconds to go until touchdown, and about 100' above the ground, a strong gust suddenly slams the airplane, lifts the right wing until we are banked about 45 degrees (or so it seems right then), we instantly drop about 50', and I make the best decision ever.

In less than a split second, I decide not to land.

With just seconds left, I level the wings, apply full power, and level the plane as I climb up and over the asphalt runway that surely would do damage to the airplane—and perhaps us as well—if I continued to the intended landing point.

My girlfriend's face is white and… frozen. Perhaps she isn't breathing. I am rather focused on controlling the airplane. With hands clamped to the armrest, at least she stops grabbing my arm!

We fly back westward over the Columbia River again. But I make a change. We both want a smoother ride for the rest of the journey.

I take the airplane up higher. About 3,000' higher, where the wind is still flowing briskly but is not so affected by the terrain. It is a smoother flight. As a side benefit, it is also a tailwind which means we are making really good time!

En route from Point A to Point B, be prepared to make adjustments to ensure Peak Performance.

In business, once up and running, unexpected circumstances sometimes demand that you make a change.

You might need to find a different price point for your product or service. Delays in vendor deliveries can cause a schedule change. You might need to make a shift in your team or staff, or you might need to fire a client!

Changes to newer technology might speed things up for you and give you a smoother ride, especially if you interface with other companies that use the newer technology.

You might need to become more—or maybe less—hands-on.

Perhaps you need to change how much attention you give to your analytics, either more or less.

You cannot afford to be rigid and inflexible, as you'll see in Chapter Eight. The person who is prepared to understand what is happening in real-time and who is flexible enough to make the appropriate changes is the one who will operate at Peak Performance.

Ancient Scripture extolls two skills:
1. Understand the times.
2. Know what you should do.

Think about that. What are the "times" you are in right now? Take some time to answer that. In your LOGBOOK or journal, take time to write down where you are experiencing "turbulence"—places and areas that are bumpy at the moment. Make a list of them.

Then, for each one, brainstorm possible changes you could make to catch a better tailwind.

Remember that the rule for brainstorming is that you only write down ideas as they come to you. You don't ask why or how or make judgments on the value or worthiness of any idea as you brainstorm and write.

Always write these things down! You won't keep them in your head, and this is too important to the successful outcome that you are after.

When you've written down as many ideas as possible, *then* go back over and figure out the pros and cons of each idea.

Sometimes, I will give each idea on the page a value of A, B, C, or D. Then I narrow the funnel and filter out the Cs and Ds.

From there, you'll have a better understanding of what to do. Make the decision to the best of your ability. And cruise at Peak Performance!

You can't change the wind.
But you can change your altitude.

Do this, and…

Pursue Peak Performance!

Chapter 7

Navigation

I had a compass from Denys, to steer by he said,
but later it came to me that we navigated differently

—Karen Blixen

D oug had a compass, but it was dark, and the weather was foggy that early July morning at Floyd Bennet Field in New York City. For the next twenty-eight hours, he flew solo in his highly modified, single-engine Curtiss Robin airplane, nicknamed "Sunshine," which for that trip carried an amazing 320 gallons of fuel.

Wrong Way Corrigan

The year was 1938, and the flight plan for the day was approved for a non-stop flight from New York back to California, retracing the flight of the week before.

Doug pointed the nose of the small but heavy aircraft straight down the 4,000-foot runway and initially headed east before climbing into the fog and clouds.

His compass was mounted on the floor of the airplane, not insignificant considering the darkness and the fuel that sloshed an inch deep on the floor due to a leaking gas tank. He could not see the compass with clarity.

Twenty-eight hours and 18 minutes later, Douglas Corrigan landed.

In Ireland.

Not California.

He claimed that it was the compass... that he had misread it... that, in fact, he was reading the wrong end of the needle. So, instead of flying west non-stop to California, he inadvertently flew east over the Atlantic, which he could not see, and landed in Dublin.

To this day, the term "Wrong-Way Corrigan" applies to someone who plans on going in one direction but accidentally goes in another.

The thing is Douglas Corrigan had the resources and experience to complete the journey—an amazing journey—entirely in the wrong direction! He just misread his compass, pointed his nose the wrong way, and landed in Ireland instead.

Compass

How about you?

Where do you want to land at the end of your journey or the end of your endeavor (or the end of next week, or month, or quarter, or year)?

You need clarity in two things, or else face an amazing journey through the next twelve months in completely the wrong direction:

1. You need to be clear on where you want to be when you land.
2. You need to be clear on the direction to get from where you are to where you want to be.

Write down your destination. Spell it out.

Re-write it until you know you can't miss it because you can see it clearly.

Then, consider all the resources you have available (gifts, talents, experiences, finances, abilities, friends and cohorts), and plan the journey from where you are to where you want to be.

Like following a map, know your directions, know each step and each waypoint, each milepost, each rest area, each gas station—so you know where you should be as you make progress toward where you want to land.

Do this for your business.
Do this for your personal journey, as well.
Be clear on your destination and direction.
Follow your compass.
Enjoy the journey!

Begin today—and celebrate the landing—exactly where you intend to be at the end.

Do this, and…

Pursue Peak Performance!

Chapter 8

Communication

---

*Feedback is the breakfast of
champions*

—Ken Blanchard

The flight is, as usual, boring. Mundane. Pretty much a snoozer. And, literally, one of my three passengers sleeps as I fly over the border from Wyoming into northern Colorado.

What else are my passengers going to do on a 4 ½-hour flight in a six-passenger, single-engine airplane where the ground slowly slides by 5,000' below, and the engine drones on and on and on. I am flying from a fuel stop at Mountain Home, Idaho, to Denver.

I am the Pilot in Command. I have everything under control. Though bored, I continue vigilance in watching for other aircraft in the air, scanning my navigation instruments and my systems indicators and...

Wait a minute.

There are two fuel gauges, one for the tank in the left wing and one for the right. I have switched back and forth from left tank to right in order to maintain a balance. The fuel gauges are on the instrument panel in front of the right seat where sits another of my bored passengers.

And both gauges read Empty!

But this shouldn't be happening! When I refueled, I personally filled both tanks and should have had enough fuel to reach Denver and still had a 45-minute reserve.

In flight training for instrument flying, I was taught, "Always trust your instruments. Except the fuel gauges." A more accurate gauge of fuel consumption is my watch because I know how much fuel my engine is burning per hour.

But still… when your fuel gauges are on Empty, it makes you wonder!

And then I suddenly stop wondering. Because the engine coughs, sputters, and dies.

The left tank is dry. I instinctively reach down to the fuel selector valve and turn it to the right tank. In the moments that follow, I watch the propeller windmill as we coast through the air, and then…

The engine starts up.

However, the right fuel gauge also shows Empty. With the left tank unexpectedly dry, I have no idea how much fuel is actually in the right tank. And I worry.

I'd been taught early on that there are three things every pilot must always remember, and especially when The Unexpected happens:

Aviate
Navigate
Communicate

…and in that order.

First, Aviate means "Fly the plane." Before I do anything else, I have to ensure that I have the airplane under control. Losing control is the number one cause of aviation accidents.

Then, Navigate. I plan how to get from where I am to where I want to be.

I need a new place to land.

Denver Approach starts vectoring me—changing the headings I fly in order to ensure spacing between myself and other airplanes and airliners who share the same airspace.

Now, I'm in a little bit of a hurry!

So, I did the third thing. Communicate.

"Denver Approach, Cessna 1065V, how long are you going to be vectoring me around? I'm a little low on fuel."

I say that without a tone, without evidence of the tension I feel... I just state the facts.

"Cessna1065V, Denver Approach. Are you declaring an emergency?"

"Negative." My engine is running. Plus, and oblivious to the danger of this, I have a case of "get-there-it is." I'm behind schedule, and people are waiting for me at the airport.

"Not yet."

Nevertheless, the controller on the ground gives me a new direction to turn... from direct south to south-southwest. He is guiding me straight to Stapleton International Airport on the other side of Denver. Stapleton International is the seventh busiest airport in the world! And I've never been there.

I watch the instruments. I pay close attention to what they tell me. They show me my altitude and my rate of descent, my airspeed, and my direction.

I listen to the controller on the radio who says things like:

"Cessna 1065V, fly heading one-six-five. Descend and maintain eight thousand feet."

"Cessna1065V, turn right, heading one-six zero. Descend and maintain seven thousand feet."

"Cessna 1065V, turn left, heading one-two-five. Maintain seven thousand."

The fuel gauge is still on empty.

On his radar, he sees exactly where I'm at, how fast I'm going, what altitude I'm at, where other aircraft are, and what terrain is around me.

He gives me instructions and feedback. All the while, I pay close attention to what my instruments are telling me.

"Cessna 1065V, do you see the airport?"

It's a late August afternoon, and my eyes strain through the smog and haze of the Denver metro area to find Stapleton on the far side of the city.

"Negative. Airport not in sight."

He is not perplexed. He keeps giving me more feedback. I keep watching my instruments.

Somewhere just north of Denver, and getting closer Stapleton, I see the airport.

"Cessna 1065V, do you see Runway 26 Right?"

I look at the airport diagram, and I see 12 different ways I can land at Stapleton. I know that Runway 26 Right means that there is at least one parallel runway called 26 Left. In fact, there is a nearly parallel Runway 25.

OK, so that's a little confusing from the air.

Stapleton International Airport – pilot's view

And still, my unseen "coach" on the ground gives me advice, guidance, and feedback. There is not a hint of criticism or frustration in his voice. He does his job of helping me, a pilot who is not yet but imminently in danger, by giving me the exact information I need to continue to my destination and, hopefully, a smooth and successful landing.

Let me leave you hanging there for just a moment...

There's a huge lesson here for business and for life. Sometimes we need feedback. Communication.

Here's the critical key to effective communication when you need feedback:

You need feedback from sources not emotionally involved.

You need feedback from sources not emotionally involved.

My instruments have no emotions. They actually don't care what I do. They just give me feedback on what I do. They tell me exactly what I need to know in the moment.

My air traffic controller is not emotionally involved. He doesn't know me—not even my name—only my aircraft number. He is seated casually and comfortably in a padded office chair in a warm building while sipping a warm cup of coffee and watching the radar monitor in front of him.

He gives me feedback I *need* to hear.

The emperor in Hans Christian Anderson's tale, *The Emperor's New Clothes*, wants feedback when he dresses himself in the new emperor suit, hot off the loom of a couple of trickster tailors. They tell him that the clothes they will make for him, should he pay them handsomely, will have two wonderful properties. First, the clothes will be so fine and light that he won't feel the fabric when he puts them on. Second, people who are incompetent or stupid won't even see the clothes! That second would be a remarkable asset when you're an emperor with a huge staff. So, he pays the tailors.

Indeed, when he dons the new clothes, he cannot feel them. And when he looks in a mirror, neither can he see them. The obvious implication is that he himself is incompetent or stupid.

Yet, with utter vanity, he calls for a huge parade down Main Street. Atop his finest carriage, pulled by his handsomest horses and attended to by his best coachmen, he parades down the street. People line up on both sides of the street to cheer and applaud the emperor.

Of course, not one of them sees anything on the emperor except his underwear, but not wanting to let on that they may be incompetent or stupid, they keep it to themselves and, wanting to make sure that those in proximity get the impression that there is not a hint of incompetence or stupidity, continue cheering all the more wildly.

And the emperor is receiving the accolades he so mega-egomaniacally desires.

Until the end of the parade.

There is a young lad, unconcerned with thoughts of incompetence or stupidity, who calls out to everyone around him, "Hey! Hey! Hey! The emperor has no clothes!"

And finally, someone tells the emperor what someone *should* have told him long ago, like before the parade was even planned, that he had been tricked. The clothes did not exist. He *really* should have gone in a different direction!

The problem is that everyone was telling the emperor what they knew he *wanted* to hear, not what he *needed* to hear. Plus, they were concerned more about their own reputations than about telling the truth.

Getting *unemotional* feedback is key. I learned this in one sentence from a staff member of the organization putting on a conference I attended years ago. I met him in the lobby, struck up a conversation, and shared with him a situation that perplexed me. He amazed me with a clear answer that fit exactly what I needed for that moment.

"How come I didn't think of that?" I asked.

He replied, "You just needed to talk with someone who isn't emotionally involved."

How about you?

The value of a business advisor or consultant is that what you don't see, they see and share with you—as an outsider, unemotionally involved, like the air traffic controller on the ground. You get advice and feedback.

At the gym, your trainer sees where you are and where you want to be and gives you the advice and feedback you need to get there.

At home, a good book on relationships can give you that outside perspective to point you in the right direction and get you through a tough spot.

Any time you want to get from Point A to Point B, my advice is to get feedback from someone outside, someone who understands where you are and where you want to be—and most importantly is not emotionally involved.

Back in the cockpit of Cessna 1065V...

The guy on the ground at Denver Approach gave me step-by-step guidance and feedback. He lined me up westbound on final approach for Runway 26 Right, and there it was... directly in front of me, now plain to see.

I landed, taxied to the refueling area, and topped off both tanks. Because I know how much fuel each tank holds, and because I know how much fuel I put in, I figure I'd had about 15 minutes left before declaring that emergency the controller asked me about.

Thanks to...

Communicate!

Do this, and…

Pursue Peak Performance!

Chapter 9
Why Wings Bend

Whatever my aptitudes or talents, becoming a proficient pilot was hard work, really a lifetime's learning experience.... Experience is everything. The eagerness to learn how and why every piece of equipment works is everything. And luck is everything, too.

—Chuck Yeager

I stand outside, looking into the huge Boeing Factory hangar at Paine Field in Everett, Washington—the largest structure under one roof in the world and the birthplace of the Boeing 767. I am a flight test mechanic on the very first 767 ever built.

Inside the structure, one of the flight test 767s is fastened into a huge jig – a device that holds the airplane body firmly in place – while the wingtips are supported from underneath by (again, huge!) jacks. The jacks have started pushing up very slowly on the wingtips, a process so slow that it will take hours.

When I check back later for another look, the wingtips are elevated much higher so that the wings themselves are now bowed up in an arc from the body, or fuselage, of the aircraft. It looks unnatural. Unbelievable, really!

This process is called a stress test and is an engineering procedure to see how much resilience the wings have before they reach the breaking point. They bend the wings up until something actually breaks or comes apart.

But before that extreme point, you should see how far those wings bend and yet are still within acceptable limits. You cannot believe how much those wings can bend and not break!

Resilience and flexibility are something you want in airplane wings. Without it, the wings actually would break.

So, when you are a passenger on an airliner, and you look out the window and notice the wings flexing some, breathe a sigh of relief. It's good and it's normal… and it's nowhere near what those wings *could* flex and still be perfectly fine.

How about you?

I'm pretty sure that you are more resilient than you think you are. Facing turbulent times may not feel comfortable, but you'll flex a lot more than you think you can.

You are more resilient than you think you are!

If your journey gets bumpy, keep flying! Make changes, if that will help.

There are certainly times when a pilot might ask Air Traffic Control for a different altitude assignment to find a less bumpy ride. That's being flexible, making a change in the process without changing the mission.

Then, there are times when a diversion may be necessary because of weather ahead that is beyond acceptable limits (see chapter on Weight and Balance). Wisdom and experience come into play here.

But when turbulent times happen to you, don't panic!

Remember your mission. Your mission in life and/or business is like a pilot's mission—to get from Point A to Point B. (see chapter on Navigation)

In spite of "Safety First" mottos, our mission is not safety. Safety is always in the context of mission. Mission and safety go hand in hand.

In flying there is a term called "get-there-it is," and it can be fatal. That's when the pilot is so concerned about getting to Point B that they forget about safety and push into places they should be turning away from—like flying into big, towering, thundery cumulonimbus clouds, or like forgetting to monitor fuel gauges in order to press on without having to stop. These do not usually have happy endings.

Not being able to flex with changing and stressful circumstances may not have a happy ending either.

Get-there-itis compromises the mission, just like impatience does in so many other personal and business endeavors. You run the risk of not getting there at all.

Get-there-itis does not let you flex when the weather ahead looks more turbulent that you want to fly in, nor does it allow you to land and refuel just because your fuel gauges are on empty. Rigidity can make things snap.

How does this apply?

Turbulence tests the flexibility and resilience of your organization (or your body, soul, and spirit). It also tests your calmness and patience, your focus, and your resistance to panic.

When I started telling people the story of my experience with engine failure over northern Colorado, early response from listeners was that I told it too calmly. They thought that having my engine quite 5,000' above the ground should create some anxiety, panic, or even terror in me.

Then I had a flash of brilliance... what do you *want* your pilot to be like? Do you want your pilot to turn to the passengers… "Aaaaaaagghh!!!? What are we going to do?????"

You want your pilot to stay calm no matter what.

And the pilot is you.

When you start bouncing around in turbulent times, remember not to panic. You are flexible and more resilient than you know.

Experience. Rely on your experience and the lessons learned *from* your experiences.

My knuckles on the controls of an airplane are no longer white, no longer in a death grip, when I fly through turbulence.

In the beginning, in those early flight lessons next to the Blue Mountains separating Pendleton and La Grande, Oregon, my instructor frequently reminded me to relax my grip on the controls. I was not yet used to the bounciness of a small airplane in turbulent air.

But over time, I saw that the airplane didn't come apart, that we didn't fall from the sky, and that we could get to where we wanted to go. Experience gave me confidence.

Get experience and learn. Then remain calm for the sake of your staff, your team, your family, and your mission.

It does help to write, so open your LOGBOOK or journal and make notes on the current situation. And write down any experiences you've had that you can draw from.

And get feedback.

It's always too soon to panic

You do what you can for as long as you can, and when you finally can't, you do the next best thing. You back up but you don't give up.

—Chuck Yeager

Do this, and…

Pursue Peak Performance!

Chapter 10
Bring It Home

"Cessna 1065V, Gray Field tower… you are cleared to land Runway 15."

The weather is perfect—a very light breeze under clear, blue Pacific Northwest skies. I am on final approach for landing in the flying club Cessna Turbo 206.

On "short final," moments away from touchdown, a final check shows me everything is fine. As the wheels gracefully contact the asphalt runway, I know this is a textbook landing. But then…

Only a few seconds after touchdown, another airplane zooms just 50 feet above me, also coming in for a landing. Right in front of me! That airplane touches down just ahead as I continue my rollout.

Instantly, I evaluate options, should I need them. Steer left? Right? I brake hard, but not so hard as to lose control.

The happy ending is that, in a few minutes, we walk away from this one. I do have words for the tower controller who had cleared the other airplane to land right in front of me.

In fairness to the other pilot, I was probably not visible from his vantage point. Or, he misunderstood the runway he was to land on. The tower controller certainly should have been paying attention! It was an error—not mine, but potentially fatal. It was a very close call, indeed!

Near miss after touchdown! Just when it seemed like the journey was over... it wasn't.

Even at the finish line, unexpected things can happen. The lesson is: You must pay attention all the way to and through Point B.

Over half of all general aviation accidents occur at takeoff or landing, and most of those are because the pilot was not paying attention to controlling the airplane.

You may be tired. You may be bored. You may have become complacent. But carry your endeavor all the way to its conclusion. Focus! Pay attention! Don't stop being alert until after you taxi in and tie down the airplane... and THEN relax!

Carry your endeavor all the way to its conclusion. Focus! Pay attention. Celebrate both your journey and the finish line.

At some point, you finish your journey. Your endeavor, or some definable segment of it, comes to its conclusion.

You, the Pilot in Command, have survived turbulent times. You walk away from a successful mission.

Some say it's the journey, not the destination, that counts.

But... running around in circles is a journey, too.

Yes, there's value in the journey. The primary value of the *journey* toward a goal is, as the late, great Jim Rohn said, "because of what it makes of you to achieve it." The process of what happens on the way, the decisions you make, the hardships you endure, the challenges you accept, the disciplines you master, all make something of you—so that in the end, should you not achieve victory, you are at least more than you were before you set out.

It is not the critic who counts, nor the man who points out how the strong man stumbled, or where the doer of the deeds could have done them better.

The credit belongs to the man who is actually in the arena; whose face is marred by dust and sweat and blood; who strives valiantly; who errs and comes short again and again; who knows the great enthusiasms, the great devotions; and spends himself in a worthy cause; who, at best, knows, in the end, the triumph of high achievement; and who, at worst, if he does fail, at least fails while daring greatly, so that his place shall never be with those cold and timid souls who know neither victory nor defeat.

—Theodore Roosevelt

I say both matter—both the journey *and* the destination. The destination is the *reason* for the journey. Do more than just run around in circles!

If you take the journey, let the endeavor make of you what it will. Turbulent times, and all. Be attentive to everything you've learned here—all the way to the finish line.

And when you get there, give thanks to your mechanic. Give thanks to your ground controllers. Give thanks to your co-pilot. Give thanks to your teammates, to your co-workers, to your friends. Give thanks to God.

Celebrate *both* your journey *and* the finish line.

Congratulations!

Celebrate Peak Performance!

Chapter 11
Conclusion

"You are cleared to land!"

Reading a book is good.
Understanding the book is better.
Implementing ideas you get from the book is best... what makes all the difference in the world!

Every journey from Point A to Point B involves risk, and you will pursue it with purpose and with a plan—and still get blindsided by The Unexpected.

Now, with the ideas you've gleaned from working through the principles in the book, you can be prepared to handle The Unexpected when it happens and handle it well so you don't crash and burn.

In the end, don't you want to do more than survive? You want to SOAR!

And you want to soar to new heights. Soar to places that are fulfilling to you and meaningful to others.

That will mean Peak Performance no matter how turbulent the times get for you.

I hope you enjoyed the stories. They're fun. I also hope you take seriously the things you've written in your LOGBOOK or journal. They're life changing.

Then, I hope you are all in for the journey ahead.

You will make a difference!

My wish for you:
Blue skies, tailwinds, and happy landings!

You will go farther, fly higher,
and last longer than you think!

P.S.
Remember to send me your story!

Go Deeper, Farther, Higher...

If you enjoyed this book, then you must get this one:

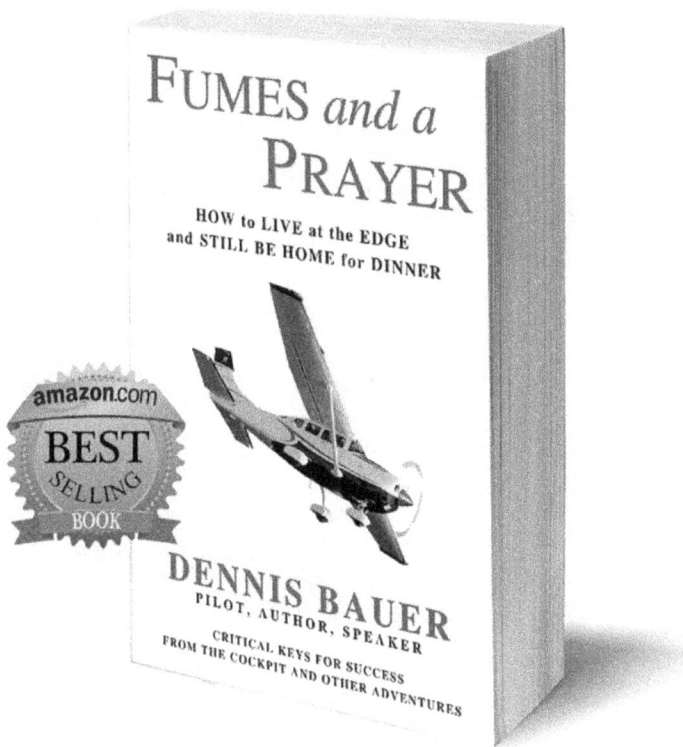

Amazon's #1 Bestseller in Leadership and Motivational/Self-Help. Get a personalized, signed copy at DennisBauer.com/book.

Imagine the next step...

Like the man I sat across from who was a successful COO of a successful chain of stores until the owner of the company sold it. **Now this man needed a change**.

In an hour of Q&A, one suggestion came to my mind, a suggestion from the world of storytelling, which is one of my areas of expertise. I offered this one idea to him.

"I never thought of that," he said. And that changed everything.

Now, for you, having me advise or consult with you could make all the difference in achieving *your* goals.

The value I bring to you and your endeavor isn't cheap, but if you can add to your bottom line, or even multiply it several times, **this could make all the difference to you**, to your hopes and dreams, and to those who are with you in your journey.

Now bring me in as an advisor or consultant. Email me at Info@DennisBauer.com.

Do more than just survive. I want you to SOAR to new heights with Peak Performance.

Speaking Engagements

Enthusiastic audiences say,

"...uncanny ability to connect with any audience."

"...You really need to have Dennis Bauer come share."

"...the most natural and engaging speaker I've seen anywhere!"

"...uplifting, motiving, and inspiring presence."

"...engaging, energetic, and a joy to listen to and learn from!"

"...Thanks for making our conference a great success!"

"...Highlight of our national conference."

From small groups to hundreds, I'm passionate about making a difference in every attendee's life. And I want you, the event planner, to look good... so every attendee says, "Thank you for inviting Dennis to speak!"

Contact me at Info@DennisBauer.com for rates and schedule, or call me at 253-681-6110.

Online courses in development...

Craft Your Story: Start to Finish

Cover-to-Cover: Your Book in Print

The Speech, The Speaker, and The Stage: How to Create
and Deliver Life-Changing Speeches

What now? Follow me at...

Facebook   - DennisBauer.com/FB

Instagram - DennisBauer.com/IG

LinkedIn   - DennisBauer.com/LI